To Paul family

What a pleasure
to have met you.

With kind regards

[signature]

London, April '96

The BEST

of

George Houghton

The BEST of

George Houghton

SEAN ARNOLD, LONDON, MAYFAIR

Published in 1991
by Sean Arnold,
Grays Antique Market,
58 Davies Street,
London W1Y 1AR

Printed by The Bath Press, Avon

© Sean Arnold

ISBN 0 9516078 2 0

PUBLISHER'S FOREWORD

Publishing a book of George Houghton's best cartoons was a positive 'must' for me. His fanatical golfers, their antics and comments have amused me for years, so I had to pass on the laughs. The uninitiated will find fresh drole humour and sometimes even a crumb of wisdom.

The drawings come from sources in many countries. Houghton was widely popular. I am delighted to be publishing one hundred selected drawings in this collection. May they give as much pleasure to you as I have had putting them together.

Sean Arnold

London

ADDICTION

by a Golf Widow

Until collectors descended on his studio in our Dorset home and bought them up, my golf-addicted husband had retained a few cartoons as his personal favourites. They had been salvaged from publishers and printers and had these drawings been available maybe they would have helped in the compilation of this book. Yet possibly not. How does one decide on cartoons? What is funny to one person may be dull to another. Hopefully readers will understand the difficulties, and just laugh their heads off.

George and I believe that Sean Arnold was the right man to publish this book. He says that he has been a Houghton fan for years, and I really think that assembling these cartoons has done him as much good as a roar of Irish laughter.

My spouse has cornered golf addiction as a theme for his cartoons. He makes a detailed study of golfing emotions, and we have both had to live with it.

Once a golf addict always a golf addict, they say. George ferrets out foibles and characteristics, draws the characters involved, and offers predicaments and comments as cartoons and to hell (he says) with anyone who takes offence.

In America, Japan, Brazil, Sweden and goodness knows where else, George finds golf addiction. Filipino Dindo Gonzalez, an acknowledged Manila golf addict, told us of a Roman Catholic priest on a remote island who used the church offertory to maintain nine holes for his flock of golf fanatics!

Fanaticism being what it is, and golf teeming with fun and belly laughs, can you wonder that my husband cartoons the game, and that it was essential to compile a book of his best efforts?

How does one select the best G.H. cartoons from thousands published and printed all over the world? My husband says he tries to portray 'inner torment'. There is plenty of that in golf.

Bing Crosby was a G.H. fan. For years he arranged that a hundred Houghton Golf Addict Cartoon Calendars should go to golfing friends all over the world. George searches out golf's inner secrets. He is shameless. In a piece about himself, he once wrote 'If you saw inside my brain when I'm playing golf you would be seasick. The grey matter is swirling in a furore of don'ts and do's, images and inhibitions . . .'

A golf addict takes his wife to Paris to see the shops, but he himself is more interested in the Arc de Triomphe and the possibility of clearing the high archway with an 9-iron shot! That made a Houghton cartoon, and there is something very familiar about the incident.

Most cartoons in this collection were drawn during my partner's prolific period in the 'sixties when he did eleven books within a decade. But years are no criterion in golf.

As this book goes to press George is nearer ninety than eighty. Nowadays his golf is what he calls a 'practice-ground-only affair'. Nevertheless, he is still much involved, painting golf scenes – mostly in Scotland – and always among golf addicts.

This collection of 100 golf laughs is entitled The Best of George Houghton. It is a safe bet that other G.H. cartoons, maybe better, will surely come to hand.

Kay Houghton

Dorset

"WE'RE BUSY AT THE OFFICE
—DON'T WORRY IF I'M LATE..."

"WE'LL JUST PLAY A FEW HOLES..."

"FORE!"

"GOSH ! — I'M EVEN SLICING IN MY DREAMS !"

"HE'S JUST WONDERING WHETHER TO HAVE A GO
WITH HIS BLASTER — OR PRETEND IT'S A LOST BALL"

"THREE EGGS AND MY DUNLOP 65!"

"—AND SUPPOSING IT GOES IN—THEN WHAT?"

"IT'S HIS BEST SHOT"

" PORT OR BRANDY, SIR ? "

"SSH—SH—SH !"

" I SUPPOSE AT TIMES LIKE THIS BOWLS
MAKES AN ALMOST IRRESISTIBLE APPEAL…"

" I WON'T BE A MINUTE "

"MEAT BALLS, MEAT BALLS, ALWAYS MEAT BALLS...
WHY CAN'T CHEF DO HIS PUTTING SOMEWHERE ELSE?"

"AWKWARD, OLD CHAP, BUT I SUPPOSE IT'S THE SORT OF THING WE MUST EXPECT IN THE AUTUMN...."

"READY, JOHNNY BOY? — DON'T MAKE
ANY PROMISES ABOUT WHEN WE'LL BE BACK!"

"THE FIRST THING IS LEARNING TO BALANCE THE BALL ON THE TEE"

"—SO PLEASE DON'T ADJUST YOUR SET"

" WEDGE "

"DOING ANYTHING PARTICULAR
THIS AFTERNOON ?"

" PLAYING SAFE, EH ? "

"NO, WE'RE _NOT_ INTERESTED IN A THREE-BALL!"

" SAY WHAT YOU LIKE, ALL I CAN HEAR
IS A SMALL VOICE WHISPERING —
'YOU'RE GOING TO FLUFF IT'... "

" CAN THIS BE THE SAME CONFIDENT CAREFREE HUSBAND WHO ONLY AT BREAKFAST TOLD ME HE HAD COMPLETELY MASTERED THE PALMER METHOD ?"

"WHAT DO YOU KNOW ABOUT FIGHTING ADVERSITY?"

" WITH A TEMPER LIKE THAT IT'S A WONDER
THE REF DOESN'T SEND HIM OFF ! "

"HE ALWAYS PRACTICES DURING SIESTA!"

"NOW, LET'S TALK ABOUT **YOU** – WHAT DO YOU THINK OF MY SHORTENED SWING ?"

"IT'S NO TIME TO MAKE 'HOLE-IN-ONE' JOKES!"

"IS THERE A GOLFER IN THE HOUSE?"

"HE'S TRYING OUT AN OVERLAP GRIP"

'THE PRO SAYS I MUST RELAX'

"I THREE-PUTTED ON SEVEN GREENS — AND WON!"

" ONE LUMP ONLY, MY DEAR "

"HE'S BROKEN THE COURSE RECORD! — FIVE PUTTS AT THE SIXTEENTH!"

" THE TIMES I'VE TOLD FRED NOT TO FINISH A SHOT ON HIS BACK FOOT ! "

"SO THAT I SHAN'T BE LATE ON THE TEE"

"THIS SHOULD BE GOOD FOR A LAUGH!"

"THERE WAS I, PLUGGED IN A DEEP BUNKER, SO ...."

"EDGAR IS GETTING FAR TOO EDGY..."

"ANY OTHER MAN CAN ENJOY A NICE QUIET
GAME OF GOLF—YOU HAVE TO HAVE A SWING THEORY!"

'QUICK! REPEAT THAT BIT ABOUT HOW
EASY IT IS TO HIT A STATIONARY BALL,
— I'M GETTING DISCOURAGED!'

"IT WENT TO THE 25th!"

" WE MUST NOW ASK OURSELVES 'DO WE REALLY
DESERVE NICE COOLING DRINKS ?'...."

"NOW, PRETEND YOU'RE SHOWING
HIM HOW TO PLAY A THREE-IRON SHOT"

" CAN'T YOU THINK OF ANYTHING BESIDES
MISSING YOUR WEEKEND GOLF ! "

"THERE WON'T BE MUCH RUN ON THE BALL TO-DAY"

" O BOY! WHAT A CHALLENGE FOR MY ACCOUNTANT!"

"MANY HAPPY RETURNS!"

"IT'S NO MORE RIDICULOUS THAN YOUR GOLF"

"QUIET PLEASE, LADIES — WE'RE BUSY"

"OH, LOOK! IT'S GONE INTO <u>MY</u> BUNKER!"

"NO THANKS, OLD MAN, I JOINED THE LEGION TO FORGET THE GAME ..."

"AH! CIVILIZATION!"

"HE'S TRYING TO PROVE THAT FROM OXFORD CIRCUS TO EROS IS A PAR FIVE"

"I WOULD SAY A SIX IRON SHOT..."

" DON'T WORRY, I'LL TAKE IT CLEAN "

'BUT COLONEL, SHOULDN'T WE FIND MY BALL FIRST,
THEN GET TO KNOW EACH OTHER BETTER?'

"HAND 'EM OVER, QUICK! — SET OF DEEP-FACED WOODS, WHIPPY SHAFTS..."

"HE INSISTED ON BRINGING THEM,
— JUST IN CASE ...."

" IF YOU DON'T WANT TO PLAY ME
WHY NOT SAY SO ?"

" DON'T FORGET YOU HAVE A STROKE AT THIS HOLE···"

" LET'S FACE IT, OLD CHAP, GOLF JUST ISN'T <u>YOU</u> "

"DON'T FORGET THERE'S A PENALTY FOR GROUNDING YOUR CLUB IN A BUNKER!"

"—AND I SAY IT WAS SHORTER THAN THE PUTT YOU MISSED
AT THE 6th.! —YOU TRYING TO START SOMETHING, FORBES?"

"GOSH! HAVE YOU EVER
SEEN A BALL WITH SUCH
A SENSE OF HUMOUR!"

" WE THOUGHT YOU WERE NEVER COMING!"

"... SO, ON THE FIFTH, HAVING A GOOD LIE, I TOOK MY BRASSIE..."

—THE OUTSIDER—

"KEEPER SAYS IT'S THE ONLY CHANCE HE GETS
TO IMPROVE HIS SHORT GAME!"

" I HAVE A FEELING THAT YOUR FRIENDS
WOULD RATHER BE SOMEWHERE ELSE…"

"WHICH OF YOU NOTICED MY DELIBERATE MISTAKE?"

" IF YOU WANT TO TELL ME ABOUT THE BIRDIE YOU'RE GOING TO GET, SPEAK IN A WHISPER— THERE'S A BEASTLY ECHO ! "

"COULD WE DISCUSS LESSONS IN TERMS OF A BLOCK BOOKING?"

"WHAT A LIFE! — FIRST MY WIFE
LEAVES ME — NOW THIS SLICE!"

" MOST ATTRACTIVE HOLE ON THE COURSE···
—THE WOODS ARE FULL OF GOLF BALLS ! "

"GUESS WHAT HAPPENED AT THE POND HOLE!"

"FOUR ROUNDS OF GOLF AT THE WEEKEND, CARPET PUTTING AT NIGHT... AND ALL YOU CAN SAY IS THAT I DON'T UNDERSTAND!"

"HE SAYS, SINCE HE HOLED IN ONE GOLF DOESN'T SEEM WORTH WHILE!"

" THERE HE GOES AGAIN ! THROWING UP GRASS TO
CHECK THE WIND... —I DON'T THINK ! "

"CAN YOU SELL ME SOMETHING
THAT WILL PUT MY OPPONENT OFF?"

"I SUPPOSE IT'S NO USE EXPECTING
YOU CHAPS TO KEEP YOUR MOUTHS SHUT"

"HE'S STILL ON ABOUT HIS FOUR AT THE FIFTH!"

"I LIKE TO REMEMBER HIM WHEN HE WAS YOUNG AND CUDDLY"

" I HATE GIMMICKS ! "

"I FANCY WE'VE GOT A REAL PROBLEM HERE, SIR"

"I THINK MY BALL IS TRYING TO
SAY SOMETHING!"

"CARPET PUTTING WILL DO FOR MOST GOLFERS —
OUR DRAWING-ROOM MUST BE A TIGER COURSE!"

"I'M BEGINNING TO THINK THAT THE TRAVEL AGENCY OVER-SOLD THIS PLACE!"

"I WOULDN'T MIND SO MUCH IF THEY CALLED THE <u>GOOD</u> PLAYERS RABBITS…"

"SOMETIMES HE PUTS *TOO MUCH* STOP ON IT"

"WATCH DADDY JUMP WHEN I REMIND HIM HE SHOULD HAVE BEEN ON THE TEE HALF-AN-HOUR AGO.."

"YOU SEEM TO THINK
I LIKE BEING A GOLF ADDICT!"

"O BOY! AM I GLAD TO SEE YOU"

" THIS IS WHERE HE MISSES IT AND BLAMES ME "

"REMIND ME TO DISCUSS THAT
ONE BACK IN THE BAR ...."

"GRIGSBY - REMEMBER ME? THINK BACK TO
GORSE HEATH ··· 1924 ··· BOYS' CHAMPIONSHIP ···"

"KEEP YOUR HEAD DOWN"

"— ABOUT THAT JUMBLE SALE ...."

"I DOUBT IF WE'LL GET ANOTHER
HOLE FROM THIS BATTERY, SIR"

"IT ONCE GOT SO ROUGH WE HAD TO
LASH OURSELVES TO TREES ... "

" YOUNG BARTLETT'S FIANCEE IS MAKING HIS GOLF INCREASINGLY DIFFICULT !"

"YOU MIGHT TRY CHALKING YOUR CLUBHEAD"

"NEXT TIME YOU WALK ROUND, FOR PETE'S SAKE **DON'T WEAR STILETTO HEELS!**"